GW00993142

Historic Troon
and its surroundings

A guide for visitors

Published by
Ayrshire Archaeological and Natural History Society
in association with Kyle and Carrick Civic Society
2011

Cover illustration: *The Kilmarnock and Troon Railway*
(Artist unknown) Courtesy East Ayrshire Council

"Like all great travellers I have seen more than I remember
and remember more than I have seen".

Benjamin Disraeli

The writers do not accept any responsibility for any accidental injury which participants might incur while following the routes described in this book.

ISBN 978-0-9564704-0-9

Printed by C & G Print, 15 Academy Street, Troon

FOREWORD

In 1998 the Ayrshire Archaeological and Natural History Society in association with the Kyle and Carrick Civic Society published a new guide book, *Historic Ayr: A guide for visitors,* which proved so popular with both residents and visitors that it sold out. A second, revised edition was produced. Recognising that it met an obvious need, the two societies decided to continue this work, and to produce similar guides to Alloway and to Prestwick.

This new volume is therefore the fourth in the series. It has been written by the team of Sheila Allan, Rob Close, Merry Graham, Sheila Penny and Stanley Sarsfield (Chairman), with illustrations specially drawn by John Doig.

We welcome the publication of *Historic Troon: A guide for visitors* and trust that readers will find that it proves to be a useful introduction to the area.

We acknowledge the help of our printers, G. Mulveny and J. Turner.

Ian Holland
President
Ayrshire Archaeological and Natural History Society

G. Michael Hitchon
President
Kyle and Carrick Civic Society

October 2011

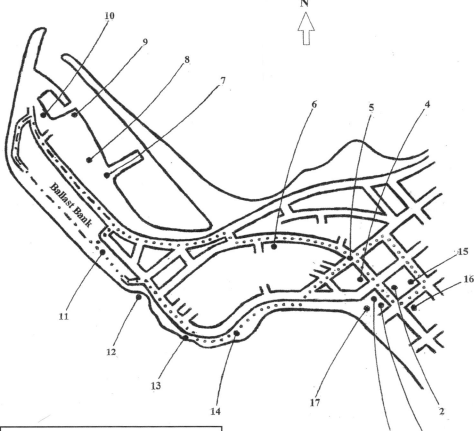

N

LEGEND

1 Car Park (Toilets towards beach)
2 Library
3 Walker Hall
4 Troon Old Parish Church
5 Troon Cross
6 Anchorage Hotel
7 Marina
8 Shipyard
9 Lifeboat Station
10 Fish Market
11 Viewfinder Cairn
12 Port Ronald
13 Betsy's Kirn
14 Italian Garden
15 St Meddans Parish Church
16 Portland Parish Church
17 War Memorial

| Trail | . . . . . . |
| Route A | . _ . _ . _ |

Approximate Scale

|_____ 1/4 mile _____|

Based on the 1909 Ordnance Survey Map

WALKING TRAIL

The trail begins at the free public car park adjacent to the Walker Hall on South Beach. There are public toilets adjacent to the car park towards the esplanade.

On leaving the car park turn left towards the town. On the opposite side of the road is the GORDON BROWN MEMORIAL GARDEN, named for Gordon L. Brown, a much-loved Scottish rugby international who grew up in Troon and was known affectionately as 'Broon fae Troon'. To the left of the garden is THE CABIN, a day centre for the elderly.

Alongside is TROON LIBRARY which was opened in 1975 and houses the M.E.R.C. (Marr Educational Resource Centre), a great resource for anyone interested in delving further into Troon's history.

On the left as you walk towards the road junction with Academy Street is the civic heart of Troon. The first building is the WALKER HALL opened in 1975 which was designed for conferences and meetings. The older building alongside is TROON TOWN HALL which was gifted to the town by Sir Alexander Walker (see page 20) in 1932. This is an impressive red brick Neo-Georgian structure containing offices of South Ayrshire Council.

It also has a galleried Concert Hall which continues to be a popular venue for dances, concerts and exhibitions and is one of the best public halls in Ayrshire. The architect was James Miller of Glasgow whose other Ayrshire designs include Turnberry Hotel and Troon railway station, which was restored a few years ago. If the Town Hall is open, take the chance to look inside.

TROON became a Burgh in 1896 having grown rapidly in the late 19th century. The economic base provided by the harbour had been boosted by the arrival of the railway in 1840, which made Troon, with its sea air, golf, and views, an attractive place to live. Many people chose to live in Troon, while working in Glasgow or Kilmarnock. By the 1890s Troon wished to have more control of its own destiny, and a number of townsmen, led by Alexander Walker, petitioned to have the town made a burgh. They were successful, and the town was to take control of many aspects of local government which previously had been the responsibility of Ayr County Council. Troon remained a burgh until 1975, when re-organisation of local government in Scotland introduced the system of regions and districts (here, Strathclyde Region and Kyle and Carrick District) which lasted until 1996, when a single unitary authority, South Ayrshire Council, was created. Like many other burghs Troon had been fiercely protective of its status, and its perceived loss in 1974-75 led to building projects such as the Walker Hall to ensure that Troon's carefully-tended money was used for the benefit of Troon and not squandered (as Troon saw it) by others.

At the road junction go straight across Academy Street. The name of the road we are on has changed from South Beach to Ayr Street which is one of the main shopping streets in Troon. The right hand side consists largely of impressive red sandstone tenements with shops on the ground floor.

Most of these tenements were built around 1900; there is a datestone high up at the junction with Academy Street. The architect-developer was Glasgow entrepreneur James Campbell McKellar. Troon has by and large escaped the homogeneous nature of many modern high streets, and still boasts a large number of locally owned businesses. Those in Ayr Street include a fishmonger and an award-winning butcher.

On the left is TROON OLD PARISH CHURCH which consists of a number of linked buildings. Originally Troon was part of the parish of Dundonald and it was only after the growth of the village in the 19th century that thought was given to establishing a church here. Troon became a separate parish in 1837. The oldest part of the complex is the church hall, which has a distinctive clock tower with an octagonal turret and spire, and is the original church of 1837 - 8. It was replaced by the much larger present red sandstone church of 1892 - 4. The architect from Edinburgh was Hippolyte J. Blanc (a Scot of French ancestry). When appointing him the congregation asked that their new church was as similar as possible to his St Matthew's Morningside (now Cluny Parish Church), Edinburgh.

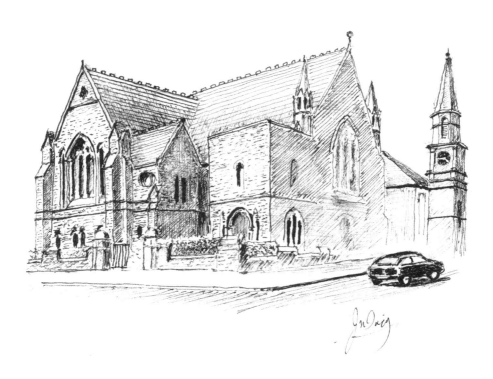

His answer was this striking design in red Mauchline sandstone, based on 13th century Gothic motifs. A proposed spire was never built, despite a bequest of £20,000 for the specific purpose of building it: the tower stump is clearly visible at the corner. A suite of halls links the two buildings. The railings around the church were put up in 1937 during the church's centenary celebrations. The church has a fine interior with barrel vaulted roofs and excellent stained glass windows. The best is perhaps the west window which depicts the Ascension of Christ. This was designed in 1903 by J. Henry Dearle, one of the chief designers with Morris & Co.

Continue along Ayr Street to the traffic lights at TROON CROSS. The road straight ahead is Templehill and the streets to right and left are Portland Street and West Portland Street.

DUKES OF PORTLAND

Although, as will be seen later, Troon had always been a harbour and a shelter for shipping, it was only in the 19th century that its potential was exploited fully, through the creation of a proper man-made harbour. In 1805 Troon was sold, along with the rest of his estate, by William Fullarton of Fullarton to William Henry Bentinck, Marquis of Titchfield. In 1795 Bentinck had married Henrietta Scott, who had inherited the Kilmarnock estates, and was known as one of the wealthiest heiresses in the country. Titchfield, who became the 4th Duke of Portland after the death of his father in 1809, set about exploiting the abundant coal reserves in and around Kilmarnock and also began seeking ways of getting the coal quickly and profitably to its markets. Ireland, which has little coal of its own, has always been a good market for Scottish coal. Initially Kilmarnock coal was brought to Troon by carts, and an ambitious plan to construct a canal from Kilmarnock to Troon foundered. After he had acquired the Fullarton estate, Portland was able to plan for the development of the harbour and the construction of a waggonway or railway to bring coal to the harbour from Kilmarnock. The harbour and the railway have had a pronounced effect on the development of Troon: both will be described in more detail later.

The 4th Duke died in 1854 and was succeeded by his eldest son, William John (1800 - 79). The 5th Duke was a "lonely, self-isolated" bachelor who seemed to have a morbid fear of contact with the rest of world. At Welbeck Abbey in Nottinghamshire, he lived in four or five rooms only, communicating with the outer world by two letter boxes, one for mail and messages in, and one out. He built tunnels under the park, including one which connected the house with the road outside the estate, allowing him to get to Worksop, the nearest town, safe and unseen when travel could not be avoided. To get to London from Worksop his carriage was placed on a railway truck, with the blinds carefully drawn.

The 5th Duke's 25 years at the head of the family mark not a time of stagnation in Troon's growth, but rather more a period of a lack of imagination and a lack of innovation. It is perhaps significant that no golf club was established in Troon until 1878, and that once under way, golf at Troon soon developed more rapidly than at Prestwick. The Dukes of Portland have had a powerful effect not only on the shape and development of Troon, but also on its nomenclature: Portland, Titchfield, Dallas, Yorke and Bentinck for instance, are all surnames which occur within the family, while Welbeck recalls their main family seat at Welbeck Abbey. The Portlands sold their Ayrshire estates in 1928.

Dorothy Cavendish, the 3rd Duke's grandmother, bought from Sir William Hamilton the blue glass Roman vase known as the PORTLAND VASE. Hamilton (the husband of Emma, Nelson's mistress) had purchased it from James Byres, a Jacobite antique dealer living in Rome, who had acquired it in 1780 in lieu of a gambling debt. The vase, which dates from about 30 BC, had previously been in the collections of Cardinal del Monte (Caravaggio's patron) and Pope Urban VII. The Duchess lent the vase to Josiah Wedgwood, whose jasperware copies ensured its enduring appeal. It is one of the best-known Roman artefacts in the British Museum.

Using the pedestrian crossing, walk up Templehill. On the left the Jade Dragon was once the celebrated TOG'S CAFÉ which was opened in the early 1900s by Giovanni Togneri from Tuscany. Further along, Brodlie's is on the site of the Pavilion cinema which became a ten-pin bowling alley in the

1950s. The castellated buildings on the other side, known as The Turrets, were built in 1893-4 for the Troon Unionist Club with the rooms for the club on the upper floor which included a billiard room and a circular reading room. The long grey sandstone terrace on the same side is known as Rome's Buildings, after the developer James Rome, a Kilmarnock builder. They were built around 1888. Back on the left-hand side of Templehill there is another building worth a look, a quirky red sandstone one with Jacobean details. Built as a bank, c.1900, it was later the town's library and is now a dental clinic.

TEMPLEHILL

Templehill gained its name from the summerhouse built around 1750 by William Fullarton, the father of Colonel Fullarton (see page 22). It was known as Fullarton's Folly or the Temple by local people. It was of classical design with a domed roof and two storeys high. It had windows all round and as it was situated on high ground, gave good views out to the Firth of Clyde. It is possible that it was used as an observatory. The interior was richly decorated, with a Latin dedication to Bacchus, the Roman god of wine - Baccho laetitiae datori amacis et otio sacrum *- which translates as 'Built to Bacchus, the giver of happiness for friends and for leisure'. When the new harbour and road were built in the early 19th century, the folly was demolished. Its precise location is unknown but it is thought to have stood close to the road junction at the Wood Gardens.*

In Templehill note that many of the houses here had cellars which were useful during the profitable smuggling trade carried out during the 18th century. Some of the houses had long front gardens with iron railings and today, while the gardens have gone and car parking has taken over some of this space, passers-by enjoy the unusually wide pavement. On the grassy open space on the right-hand side of the road, there is a small shelter surmounted by a clock. This shelter contains information boards telling the history of Troon's lifeboats, shipbuilding and the Kilmarnock and Troon Railway. Further along the ANCHORAGE HOTEL was originally the Portland Arms Hotel and the terminus for the coaches bringing passengers to and from the first Troon railway station in Dundonald Road, which opened in 1816. The hotel is the oldest licensed premises still in use in Troon and also dates from 1816. Alongside the Anchorage and forming an impressive little group, are a number of other classical villas from the early years of the 19th century. These were mostly the summer homes of wealthy Kilmarnock merchants who sent their families here for the summer to engage in the fashionable activity of sea-bathing. The gentlemen usually joined their families at weekends.

KILMARNOCK AND TROON RAILWAY

The first railway to be constructed in Scotland under an Act of Parliament, the Troon railway was the idea of the 4th Duke of Portland, who commissioned William Jessop to survey the route, which ran from Kilmarnock through Drybridge and Barassie, to the terminus at Troon. The line was planned to carry coal from Portland's mines around Kilmarnock to Troon harbour for onward shipment to Ireland. Construction began in 1808 and the line opened on 12th July 1812; the trains of waggons were pulled by horses. The line carried passengers from 1814. Three years later the first steam railway locomotive in Scotland, a George Stephenson design, was employed for trials on the line. In 1820 another steam locomotive, The Duke, entered service, and remained in service until 1848. A silver model of The Duke is at Rozelle House, Ayr.

The largest surviving part of the line is the four-arch viaduct over the river Irvine at Laigh Milton. This is the oldest river-spanning railway bridge in the world, and is visited on the car trail (see page 30).

Again continuing along Templehill, turn right at the next turn in the road, just before the small formal garden. Walk along the paved path beside the garden which, so a plaque tells us, is 'Ground Improvement gifted to the Community in 1914 by Adam Wood Esq. of Skeldon'. Wood was a coal owner and also manager of the Ailsa Shipyard, who lived in Portland Villa in Templehill, just beyond the garden on the left side of the road. He was a noted philanthropist and after his death his home became the Wood Memorial Miners' Welfare Home. The Home has been demolished and modern housing built on the site. The trail continues on the left-hand side of Harbour Road crossing Garden Place where you can see on the other side of the road the entrance to the Troon Cruising Club. Cross Kennedy Road and further along on the other side of Harbour Road there are some unusual paving stones at the entrance to Troon Yacht Haven which opened in 1978 in the well-sheltered inner basin of the harbour. It is used by many sailing boats both large and small and is popular with yachtsmen as the waters in this area are among the best for racing in Europe. This marina covers around five acres of land and 18 acres of water, with berths for 300 boats. In December 2003 Associated British Ports sold Troon Marina to Yacht Havens Group for £1,500,000. Facilities include Scott's, a restaurant which is open to the public. Some tables have good views.

One of the main movers in the establishment of the marina was SIR ROBIN KNOX JOHNSTON. He was the first person to sail round the world singlehanded and nonstop in 1969. Over the years he has gained many honours including a knighthood in 1995 and has been the United Kingdom's Yachtsman of the Year three times, a unique achievement. Among his business interests was the development of marinas, in particular those at Troon and St. Katherine's Dock in London.

Continue along Harbour Road till you reach Craig Road - here you now have a choice:

The harbour area is quite busy with timber lorries and many areas are restricted. This can be quite a challenging walk which is particularly bracing on a cold windy day but it can be rewarding if you are interested in Troon's historic harbour. To do this continue along Harbour Road and follow Route A.

Alternatively turn left into Craig Road. Climb up the path to the top of the Ballast Bank, with views over the Firth of Clyde and the marina and sawmill. Turn left and walk along some distance to the viewfinder cairn which will be on your right where you rejoin Route A (page 13).

Route A continues along the left-hand side of Harbour Road, almost immediately across the road is the entrance to James Fleming's yard where can be seen a plaque commemorating the Kilmarnock and Troon Railway.

TROON HARBOUR

Geography dictates that the sea has always played a major role in the history of Troon. This was evident as early as 1608 when the Burgh of Irvine, motivated by the silting up of the mouth of the River Irvine, gave permission for a new harbour to be built at the 'Trone'. In 1688 the Tobacco Lords of Glasgow saw the advantages of this site but were unsuccessful in acquiring this harbour and had to settle instead for a site near Greenock, which became Port Glasgow. At the time of the Act of Union in 1707 Queen Anne granted the Port of Troon a Charter as a free seaport and harbour. Troon had long been famous for its natural harbour but in 1808 the Duke of Portland spent £500,000 in improving it. A wet dock was cut out of solid rock to complement the inner and outer harbours. There were two dry docks, one to suit comparatively small coasting vessels and another to accommodate foreign-going ships which required greater depth. A long breakwater running roughly north and south protected the outer harbour. This breakwater when constructed incorporated an existing artificial island known locally as St. Helena, as it was likened to Napoleon Bonaparte's final captivity on an island of that name in the mid-Atlantic.

During the 1870s Troon was a major coal shipping port for the west of Scotland and in one year 600,000 tonnes of coal were handled. The pleasure steamers for which the west coast became famous called at Troon from 1898. In 1901 the Duke of Portland sold the harbour to the Glasgow and South-Western Railway Company. During the First and Second World Wars the harbour was used as a naval refuelling base because the depth of the water in the outer harbour allowed small and medium sized ships to get in and out at all states of the tide. The harbour is now operated by Associated British Ports.

Troon's harbour is relatively small and was originally built to take sailing ships which are small by today's standard. In its heyday, this harbour was so busy and full of shipping that one could cross from one side of the harbour to the other, walking over ships' decks. Today the harbour's facilities include a car ferry to Northern Ireland and a fish market, as well as the marina that we have already seen.

You will pass an old brick-built engine shop on your left. This, and the sandstone main offices opposite, built in 1910, are the major remaining buildings of the former Ailsa Shipyard which closed in 2004.

SHIPBUILDING IN TROON

Shipbuilding began in Troon about 1808-10, and was associated with the Duke of Portland's creation of the harbour. Around 1850 it was in the hands of the Portland Shipbuilding Company, and in 1866 it passed to the Troon Shipbuilding Company with whom it remained until 1886. During these years the yard built wooden ships, including the 'Pantaloon', for the Duke of Portland, launched in 1831. "We understand" the local press said, "she is intended for pleasure, and will carry fourteen guns." In 1886 the lease of the yard passed to Messrs McCredie and Wallace - the Ailsa Shipbuilding Company - and the buildings were considerably reconstructed.

The woodyard on the left side of the street can be better seen from further along the trail and will be mentioned later. Carry on past the woodyard and on the right there is a sign for the Lifeboat Station. Cross the road carefully and walk down towards the Lifeboat Station. The road borders the harbour wet dock where fishing boats and other smaller craft moor. Take great care to keep well clear of the edge of the basin.

LIFEBOATS

In 1871 Troon's first Lifeboat Station was established in Portland Street at the request of the local inhabitants. The first lifeboat was a 32 feet long, 7½ feet wide rowing boat with 10 oars double banked. The Duke of Portland granted a site for the lifeboat house costing £250. The Glasgow and South-Western Railway carried the first lifeboat, the Mary Sinclair, free of charge from Carlisle. In August 1886 a new self-righting lifeboat, the Alexander Munnoch, was drawn through Troon from the railway station to the harbour by "gaily decorated horses with banners flying and bands playing." The first self-righting lifeboat was from a design by James Beeching (1788-1858) of Great Yarmouth who was awarded a Medal and a Certificate at the 1851 Exhibition. In June 2004 the present lifeboat, the tenth, was launched. Named Jim Moffat, she is a Trent Class lifeboat, costing £1,300,000, has a 1,750 horsepower engine, can travel at 25 knots, and is equipped with all the latest technology.

The RNLI's Silver Medal has been awarded twice to Troon crewmen: firstly in 1941 to William McAuslane, for the rescue of seven men from the Moyallen of Belfast in December 1940 (for which Albert J. Ferguson also received a Bronze Medal), and again in 1980, to Ian Johnston. In September of that year coxswain Johnston and his crew went out in the Connel Elizabeth Cargil in poor visibility, a force 10 gale and 15-20 foot waves. Five times the lifeboat approached the dredger Holland 1 off Irvine Harbour and each time brought a crewman to safety. Troon Lifeboat Station can be visited by prior arrangement with the coxswain, and has occasional open days.

On the adjacent side of the dock is the fish market. The fishing fleet and fish market moved to Troon from Ayr in 1996 when a fish market was built to comply with new EU standards of hygiene. Berthing facilities are available for fishing vessels up to 50 feet in length and the harbour basin itself accommodates smaller boats. At times the wet dock can be a hive of activity with fishing boats entering and leaving, fish being landed and men busy mending nets. Seals and eider ducks can often be seen.

THE SCOTIA EXPEDITION

Led by the naturalist Dr William Spiers Bruce, the Scotia expedition left Troon in November 1902 on a highly successful 20-month voyage to the South Atlantic. The Scotia was a former whaler, converted at the Troon shipyard. The captain was Thomas Robertson, a Dundonian with experience of high latitude navigation. The ship's complement included a zoologist, meteorologist, botanist, bacteriologist, geologist, taxidermist and a piper. The expedition was funded largely by Andrew Coats, of the Paisley thread manufacturing family, who donated £11,000, and after whom Bruce named part of the Antarctic mainland that they reached, Coats Land.

The trail returns to the main road and goes right continuing until you reach a line of single storey cottages where our trail turns left. You can if you wish, go right and walk across to the dock and MacCallum's Oyster Bar, a popular seafood restaurant and take-away venue (The Wee Hurrie) in a former ice-making plant. Here you can see the lighthouse at the pier head and another on the breakwater built in 1889. The harbour also had a foghorn whose hoarse utterances during a fog caused it to be known locally and affectionately as the 'Trin Coo'.

Back to the trail which passes along the front of the single storey cottages which are now mostly used for commercial purposes, including a shipping agency. It then turns left, where there is a cast iron capstan, marked Clarke Chapman & Co. The road gradually becomes a path with parking areas on the right at the end of which an anchor has been set up. There are excellent views across the Firth of Clyde to Arran and Lady Isle (see page 35) and this is a favourite spot for birdwatchers.

The path climbs up to the top of the BALLAST BANK. The Ballast Bank had its beginnings in the early years of the 19th century. It is an impressive man-made mound built up over many years which was initially formed using the spoil from the Wet Dock and the new harbour. Subsequently, it was increased in size by the ballast of earth and stones brought in by ships, mostly from Ireland, calling at Troon to collect cargoes of coal and timber. The Ballast Bank gives protection to the harbour area from the predominant south-westerly winds. It is a popular walk and provides wonderful views.

On the left side of the Ballast Bank is the woodyard of Adam Wilson & Sons, still one of the largest timber merchants in the west of Scotland. The founder, Adam Wilson (1823-98), originally specialised in pit-props, and built his first modern timber yard at Auchinleck before moving to Troon in 1888. The yard and the processes involved can be observed from the Ballast Bank.

Look out for the round cairn-like viewfinder on your right which identifies points of interest over the Firth of Clyde. It was donated by Troon Community Council in 1983. THE TWO ROUTES JOIN HERE.

At the far end of the bank, the path descends gradually into Titchfield Road. Follow this road round to the right, with the sea on your right. The small inlet at the foot of the bank is called Port Ronald, where smugglers used to operate.

SMUGGLING

The west coast of Scotland had been engaged in the smuggling trade well before the Act of Union in 1707. Smuggling continued to flourish here throughout the 18th century and into the 19th century despite the setback the 'free traders' received in 1765 when the Isle of Man was sold to the British Government. The proximity of this privately owned island, which had played a key role in the trade due to its independence from British excise laws, had been to Troon's great advantage. Troon had the additional benefit of providing shelter from the prevailing winds and in 1805 it still had the largest trade in smuggling in the west of Scotland. This coincided with Napoleon Bonaparte forbidding any legal trade between European ports in his empire and Great Britain.

The ships landed at Barassie Burn (to the north of the harbour) at full tide and when the tide fell the cargo was unloaded to carts and packhorses and taken inland. Smaller ships also landed at Port Ronald at the south end of the Ballast Bank. Contraband came from the Low Countries and France, including brandy, tobacco, tea and salt. Other contraband trade involved home-made whisky from the Highlands. Often when the soldiers confiscated goods they in turn would be attacked by the smugglers to regain them. In the case of tea, this certainly was not for their own personal consumption as the farm workers in the area saw it as a drink only for those who could 'afford to be weak, indolent and useless' [John Galt, Annals of the Parish]. Farmers provided horses and goods were taken via Stewarton or Beith to Glasgow and Edinburgh.

It is said that the excise men and soldiers stationed at Irvine and Ayr were kept very busy trying to catch these smugglers. Stories have been told of young people being used as lookouts when ships with illicit cargo were being unloaded during daylight hours. They were stationed along the sand dunes on the shore to warn of the approach of the Revenue men and the Redcoats. The children would wave their shawls along the line to warn the smugglers to hide the contraband. This was often hidden in deep pits, called 'brandy holes', under some of the older houses in Troon and in the farm fields. In addition, several houses at Loans had double walls in the lofts where casks were hidden. Churches and schoolhouses were rarely searched as these were occupied by 'gentlemen', but some of these gentlemen were tempted by liquid bribes. Pulpits and graveyards as far away as Prestwick and Monkton were believed to be used as hiding places, while it has been alleged that even major landowners in this area benefited.

Those involved in the trade were often romanticised as strong, courageous and at times chivalrous. In past times, excise laws were also regarded as unjust and tyrannical and it was therefore an achievement to evade them. However, it is to be remembered that many people were corrupted by the trade through bribery or over-consumption of the goods themselves. Some smugglers were caught and a few were hanged but for the most part there were few informers and most escaped punishment.

Further on, BETSY'S KIRN is an inlet in the rocks, roughly opposite the end of Welbeck Crescent, and the scale of the Ballast Bank is best seen from here. The name is thought to derive from Betsy Miller (1792 - 1864), from Saltcoats, who for almost 50 years captained the brig Clytus, a small cargo vessel which exported coal from Ayrshire to Ireland. She took over command after her father became ill, and was the first woman to be recorded as the captain of a ship in the British Register of Tonnage at Lloyds. It is possible that she used the inlet for loading or unloading her cargoes of coal and ballast. In later years, even until the 1950s, this was a popular place with local people for swimming, with a springboard attached to the rocks and a shelter used for changing. As Titchfield Road bends gently to the left, it is possible to continue along the top of the sea wall, and drop down into a broad parking area. This was the site of Troon's OPEN AIR SWIMMIMG POOL, opened in 1931. The design of the building was influenced by the Art Deco movement and the pool was very popular with local people and holidaymakers. Every summer for many years, Archie McCulloch, who was a well-known personality, hosted a beauty contest there. During the Second World War, the commandos, who were based at Troon for a number of years, used the pool for training purposes. The pool closed in the 1970s and was subsequently demolished. The trail continues through a sunken garden, which is all that remains of the lovely ITALIAN GARDEN which was part of the pool surroundings.

Proceed along the promenade until you see West Portland Street on your left. It is before the paddling pool and the family-friendly children's play area with the crazy golf course. Descend the steps here and taking care, cross over Titchfield Road. You will see an obelisk of Portland granite within a triangular grass space. This was a Drinking Fountain which was gifted to the people of Troon in 1891 by James Dickie. He was a Glasgow builder, who was also the first captain of Troon Golf Club when it was inaugurated in 1878. He also presented the Dickie Cross, a medal which is still played for annually. Continue along West Portland Street passing on the left Rossi's Beach Café and on the right the old Bethany Hall, built 1843, and now Seagate Evangelical Church. Proceed to the crossroads.

Go across at the lights into Portland Street; on the left you will pass a brick-built housing development with a tiled entrance which used to be part of the Embassy cinema. On the right, you will see the old Co-operative store at No 30-32, with the clasped hands carved in stone high on the wall. Further on the right is located the Tesco store which used to be the Picture House, Troon's third cinema. Turn into Church Street and walk on past the impressive red sandstone former Post Office building on the right. At the junction with Academy Street, continue straight ahead. The modern St Patrick's Primary School (on the site of the town's first Catholic Church) is on the right in Academy Street and the site of the original Troon Academy, built in 1840, is on the opposite side of the street. The next junction is marked by ST MEDDAN'S PARISH CHURCH, a large red sandstone church of 1889 by John B. Wilson of Glasgow, and built for a United Presbyterian congregation, at a time when Troon was growing rapidly. Its tower and broach spire form a prominent landmark, while the highlight of the galleried interior is the stained glass in the south window, of 1892 by William Smith of London. If the church office is open, it is usually possible to gain access to the interior.

Turn right into St Meddan's Street. Further along on the left is another of Troon's churches: PORTLAND PARISH CHURCH, of 1913 - 14 by Harry Clifford. The light brown sandstone comes from Lanarkshire. The interior is particularly attractive, with many Arts and Crafts details. Again, access is usually possible if the church office is open. At the junction with South Beach, carefully cross the road, returning to the car park whence the trail started. One short loop remains: on the seaward side of the car-park are the public toilets and, a little to their north, between the Walker Halls and the sea, the town's WAR MEMORIAL. This is a prominent and imposing landmark, unveiled in 1924 and consists of a bronze statue of Britannia on a granite pedestal. Britannia stands with victory in her hand, with the chains of bondage snapped, while she holds out the palm to those of her sons who lie beyond the seas. The sculptor was Walter Gilbert.

VEHICULAR TOUR OF THE AREA AROUND TROON

Start at the car park at the Walker Hall (see description in Walking Trail, preface). Drive out of the car park and immediately stop at the junction with South Beach. When safe go straight ahead into St Meddan's Street, with the Portland Church on your right. At the next junction, marked by St Meddan's Church, turn right into Bentinck Drive. This is one of Troon's major residential areas, lined with spacious villas from the years on either side of 1900. Bentinck Drive gets its name from an ancestor of the Duke of Portland's family. Hans William Bentinck was Dutch and a life-long friend and political ally of William of Orange. In fact he is credited with arranging William's marriage to Mary, the daughter of the future King James II (VII of Scotland). One of Bentinck's rewards for his loyalty to William was the title of the Earl of Portland.

Just beyond Yorke Road (the third road on the right) is the white-harled Welbeck House, built in 1910-12, one of the grandest houses in Troon. It

was for many years a hotel, and is now a nursing home.

Just beyond, also on the right hand side, is ST NINIAN'S EPISCOPAL CHURCH, which can be recognised by its wooden lych gate.

This Arts and Crafts Church was built to designs of the accomplished Ayr architect James A. Morris. The nave was built in 1912, and the church was completed in 1921. It is in Morris's preferred red Mauchline sandstone, has a highly decorative interior and is usually open during daylight hours. There is attractive stained glass and high quality wooden furnishings. Much of the woodwork, including the Bishop's Chair and main door, was carried out by the Yorkshire wood carver Robert 'Mouseman' Thompson (1867 - 1955). Eight of his distinctive carved mouse signatures can be seen in the church. The lych gate is another work by Morris and was a gift to the church from the Duke of Portland.

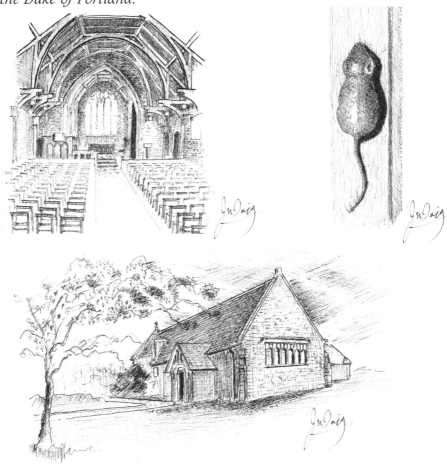

Continue along Bentinck Drive, which is still lined with attractive villas. On the right, and set well back, is Sandilands, built in 1920 - 22 by Alexander Walker for his retired employees. It is again Arts and Crafts, and the architect was James R. Johnstone of Troon, who may also have been the architect for Welbeck House. At the junction with Craigend Road, and again taking care, go straight ahead into Crosbie Road, lined with golf courses and large villas.

On the left hand side is the Portland Course used by Troon Ladies' Golf Club. The architect for this, and for the original Troon clubhouse, was Harry Clifford. Troon Ladies' Golf Club was founded in 1882 and its clubhouse officially opened by the Duchess of Portland in 1897. For many years it was one of the few ladies' golf courses in existence.

The road ends at a barrier, beyond which is a road on to the golf course. The last house is SUN COURT, originally a private house, for many years a hotel, and now a nursing home. There is a large building in the back gardens of the Sun Court which was a REAL TENNIS COURT.

Real tennis (also called Royal or Court tennis) is one of the oldest racquet games. It probably began as a hand ball game and evolved over several centuries. The game has changed little since the 17th century when it was the sport of choice for the nobility throughout Europe. The court was built in the early 20th century for the owner J. O. M. Clark, of the Paisley thread manufacturing company, but is no longer in use. The only other real tennis court in Scotland is at Falkland Palace in Fife, where the game is still regularly played.

Turn here, and return along Crosbie Road. On the left, wholly surrounded by the golf course, is BLACKROCK HOUSE, once visited by the renowned film actress Greer Garson. Further along on the left is the very prominent MARINE HOTEL. This imposing hotel, designed to cater for the many people who came to Troon to enjoy golf, was opened in 1897 and has been extended many times.

At the junction with Craigend Road, this time turn left, passing the Clubhouse of ROYAL TROON GOLF CLUB. As the road turns to the right, take the junction on the left into the South Beach Car Park.

N

Firth of Clyde

River Irvine

17

A759

18

19

Dundonald

20

Barassie

Symington

21

Loans

22

8

9

7

Start   1

10

Irvine

A77

2

12

6

11

5

Ayr

4   3

Prestwick

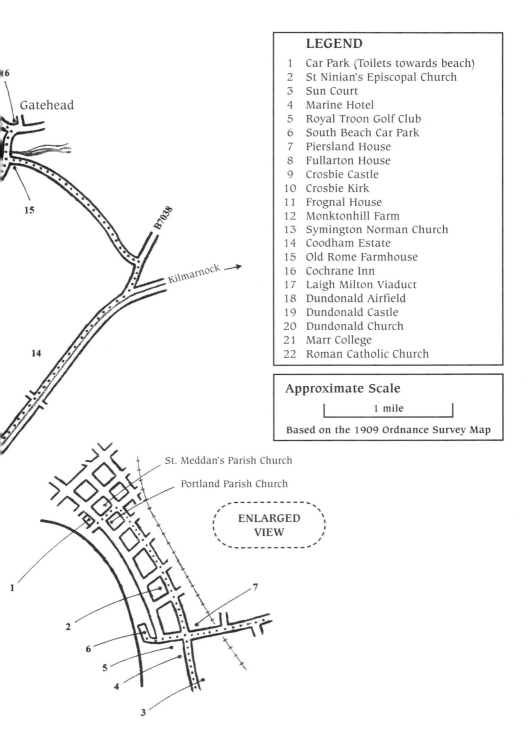

Gatehead

LEGEND

1 Car Park (Toilets towards beach)
2 St Ninian's Episcopal Church
3 Sun Court
4 Marine Hotel
5 Royal Troon Golf Club
6 South Beach Car Park
7 Piersland House
8 Fullarton House
9 Crosbie Castle
10 Crosbie Kirk
11 Frognal House
12 Monktonhill Farm
13 Symington Norman Church
14 Coodham Estate
15 Old Rome Farmhouse
16 Cochrane Inn
17 Laigh Milton Viaduct
18 Dundonald Airfield
19 Dundonald Castle
20 Dundonald Church
21 Marr College
22 Roman Catholic Church

Approximate Scale

1 mile

Based on the 1909 Ordnance Survey Map

B7038

Kilmarnock →

St. Meddan's Parish Church

Portland Parish Church

ENLARGED
VIEW

ROYAL TROON GOLF CLUB

This, the first Golf Club in Troon, was formed in 1878 and grew rapidly. The first clubhouse was a railway carriage: the present clubhouse was opened in 1886. The original course is now the Old Course. A second course, the Portland, was established in 1895: after St Andrews, Troon became the second club in Scotland to have two courses. The clubhouse has been extended several times: almost immediately after it was opened in 1889, most notably in 1905 when it was almost doubled in size, in 1926 when the colonnaded curved porch was added, and most recently in 2004-06.

The Open has been held at Troon on eight occasions (1923, won by Arthur Havers; 1950, Bobby Locke; 1962, Arnold Palmer; 1973, Tom Weiskopf; 1982, Tom Watson; 1989, Mark Calcavecchia; 1997, Justin Leonard; 2004, Todd Hamilton). Formerly known as Troon Golf Club, it was honoured with Royal approbation in 1978, its centenary year. The green-painted wooden building just inside the grounds of the golf club is an original starter's hut.

SOUTH BEACH CAR PARK

The beach and dunes at this car park give an excellent impression of the work of the Troon Dune Restoration Project in conserving and stabilising the sand dunes. Looking back towards the town there is a good view of the area covered on the walking tour. This area is very popular with dog walkers and wind surfing enthusiasts. To the south the BLACK ROCKS can be seen at low tide. In the past this was the scene of various shipwrecks and it was also a popular area for smugglers during the 18th and 19th centuries to unload their illicit cargoes of rum, tea, lace and salt. From here it is possible to follow the SMUGGLERS' TRAIL to Dundonald Castle. A notice board gives further information, and leaflets are available at Troon Library and Troon Post Office.

From the car park, turn right into Craigend Road. Beyond the junction with Bentinck Drive, and set back on your left, is PIERSLAND HOUSE HOTEL, originally a private house, built for Sir Alexander Walker in 1899 by the Glasgow architect William Leiper. This fine Arts and Crafts house remained the family home until 1956.

SIR ALEXANDER WALKER was the grandson of the founder of the famous Kilmarnock whisky blending firm Johnnie Walker. He was Managing Director of the company and created the famous Johnnie Walker Red and Black Labels. He was born in 1869 and died in 1950. Sir Alexander was a prominent member of the community and a generous benefactor to Troon. One notable, and indeed notorious, friend of Alexander Walker was Joachim von Ribbentrop, who was Hitler's Foreign Minister from 1938 until the defeat of the Germans in 1945. In 1919 von Ribbentrop had been running a wine and spirit distribution company owned by his father-in-law and had met and become friendly with Alexander Walker. He acted as Walker's agent in Germany and the two men shared the same interest in dogs. During the 1930s von Ribbentrop was Germany's Ambassador in London, and on at least one occasion flew to Troon to visit the Walkers at Piersland House, landing his plane on the golf course in front of the house. After he was hanged for war crimes in 1946 the Walkers remained in contact with his widow.

Pass Piersland House and continue straight ahead, observing the 30mph speed limit, over the railway bridges. There are now golf courses on either side of the road. This road was once known as the Danderin': Sundays saw families out and about sitting, walking, chatting to friends or just taking the air, 'danderin' in the shade of the trees. Follow the main road and as it turns right, indicate and turn left into the narrow Isle of Pin Road. After a few hundred yards you will see on the right, close to the roadside, an ancient pillar known as the Pin where it is thought that the Fullartons once dispensed justice. At the top of Isle of Pin Road follow the road, with Marr Rugby Club on the right, and continue straight ahead with the former stables of Fullarton House (now residential) also on the right, to the car park at Fullarton Park.

(There are public toilets adjacent to the car park).

WILLIAM FULLARTON was born at Fullarton House in 1754. He was a very able young man and at the age of 21 was appointed Principal Secretary of the British Embassy to the Court of France. Five years later, in 1780, at his own expense, he raised the 98th Regiment of Infantry of which he was Colonel and in 1783 he was given command of the Southern Army of over 13,000 men in the Indian subcontinent. He fought highly successful campaigns that year and the one following, which owed a great deal to his brilliant strategy. On his return to Britain he published "A View of the English Interest in India", which included an account of these campaigns. In 1793 during the war against the French he again raised troops. This time it was the 23rd Light Dragoons, which was known as Fullarton's Light Horse, and also the 101st Regiment of Infantry. Their barracks were at the top of Willockston Road. The officers' polo ground which was behind the barracks is now the Fullarton Golf Course and the ground used by the soldiers became the Municipal Golf Course. In 1793 he also published a treatise on agricultural improvements in Ayrshire (which was republished in 2002 by the Ayrshire Archaeological & Natural History Society as Ayrshire in the Age of Improvement).

Later that same year he was appointed Governor of Trinidad. On his return in 1803, he accused Sir Thomas Picton the previous Governor, of allowing a female slave to be tortured, which led to Picton being tried, but acquitted. Fullarton died in London in 1808 and was buried in Isleworth. As he had no son, his estate passed to his second cousin, Colonel Stuart Murray Fullarton, who was also his son-in-law, as he had married Rosetta, Fullarton's natural daughter, in 1796. Robert Burns knew William Fullarton and held him in high esteem as may be seen from these words written in 1785:

> Who called on Fame, low standing by, To hand him on,
> Where many a patriot, name on high, and hero shone.

FULLARTON ESTATE

This land was owned by Fullartons for around 600 years. The early family members were probably of Norman origin and the first record of the name is Alanus de Fowlerton who died in 1280. The name is thought to have been derived from their role as king's fowlers who provided game and wild fowl for the court, and this is reflected in their coat of arms which shows a hawk above three otters.

In 1707 a charter was granted by Queen Anne designating these lands "the Barony of Fullarton." It also enabled Fullarton to collect taxes from all ships anchoring there. Fullarton House was built in 1745. It was altered and extended in 1792 by the Adam brothers who also designed a new stable block. As a result of financial difficulties, Colonel Fullarton sold the estate and Troon harbour in 1805 to the Marquis of Titchfield, who later became the 4th Duke of Portland.

Fullarton House was bought by Troon Town Council in 1928 and was let as flats until it was demolished in 1966. The stable block still exists as an attractive courtyard development of private houses from the 1970s. In 1996 the gate pillars were restored and replaced in their original position and can be seen on the north side of the estate. Nearby are the remains of Crosbie Castle, which was the family home until Fullarton House was built. In the late 19th Century the vaulted ground floor room was converted into an icehouse. At the rear of the car park there is a marriage lintel from Crosbie Castle with the date 1673 and the initials WF for William Fullarton and AB which stood for Anne Brisbane, his second wife.

Among the facilities which can be enjoyed are picnic spots, pony tracks, a play area for children and woodland walks which are very popular. There is a large car park and the paths are mostly manageable by wheelchair users. Different types of trees including beech, oak, horse chestnut and Sitka spruce are to be found, and a variety of bird life and small mammals. It has been the home of Marr College Rugby Football Club since 1935.

Return to the junction and turn left, with the stable block on your left and rugby club on your right. At the next junction, turn right and continue until Crosbie Churchyard appears on your right. Park in front of the churchyard.

CROSBIE KIRK

This church dates from 1681 and was built on the site of an earlier church dating from about 1229. In 1681 a small hamlet surrounded the church. Crosbie parish was united with that of Dundonald in 1688, and the church was little used thereafter. Severe storms on 25th January 1759 - the same day as Robert Burns was born in Alloway - resulted in the roof being blown off and the gable end damaged. In 1862 Troon Cemetery was opened and Crosbie Kirkyard was no longer Troon's main burial ground, though some gravestones are of later dates.

In 1761 a Janet McFadzean was buried in Crosbie Kirkyard. The front of the gravestone reads:
"Here lyes the corps of Janet McFadzean, spous of William McFadzean, Quarter-master Sergean in Lovetenan General Homs Regiment of Sol, who died August 22, 1761, aged 27 years.

> Twenty-four years i lived a maiden life
> And three years i was a married wife
> In which time i lived a hapie life
> I trevld with him from toun to toun
> Until by death i was cut down.
> In my sister's hous did die,
> And here at Crosbie Kirk i ly,
> Where i my rest and sleep will take,
> Until at last i be awaked.
> It will not be with tuk of drim,
> But it will be when the trumpet sound,
> And while ile my Redeemer see,
> Who shed his preshios blood for me."

The entrance to the Wrack Road can be seen from the front of the Kirkyard looking towards the main road on a line with the front wall of the graveyard and, to its left through the trees, Frognal House.

SOUTHWOODS

Before the First World War large suburban houses in spacious grounds were being built in the Southwoods area for rich businessmen and industrialists. The English vernacular style Frognal is one such, built of honey-coloured sandstone for the Hart family by the Kilmarnock architect James Hay. The last family to live at Frognal were the Crystals, and it then became a Children's Respite Home, run by Glasgow Corporation, and is presently in private ownership. There are a number of other impressive houses within the Southwood area - on either side of the road which runs from Frognal back towards Troon. Some can be seen from the road, while others can be glimpsed from the WRACK ROAD, which was the track used by Fullarton estate farmers to collect sea weed (wrack) as fertiliser, and was also the main approach to Crosbie Kirkyard for funerals from Troon. This path, part of the Smugglers' Trail (see page 20) leads back to Royal Troon Golf Course, and because of its unspoiled tranquillity, a variety of wildlife and woodland plants can be seen along the path.

From the churchyard continue along the road, with the houses on your right, and at the next junction, turn left. Follow this road past Monktonhill Farm on the left, which once belonged to the Scottish Co-operative Wholesale Society, and supplied produce - especially milk and milk products - to their stores throughout Scotland. The road continues until it meets the major A79 road. Turn left onto this dual carriageway and when safe to do so immediately move into the right-hand lane and at the Monktonhead roundabout follow the road markings for the A77 (third exit, signed to Ayr, Kilmarnock, Glasgow). Move to the inside lane on this road and at the Dutch House roundabout take the first exit for the A77 Kilmarnock. After a mile or so, the entrance to Hansel Village can be seen on the right hand side.

HANSEL VILLAGE is a community which seeks to give as normal a life as possible to people with learning difficulties. It is based around an attractive house of 1933, known originally as Broadmeadows, which was gifted by Mrs Isobel Murdoch in 1962. There is living accommodation as well as a hall and other community facilities and opportunities for employment are provided.

At the signpost for Symington turn left into Symington Road South. This area was once known as Jeanfield Toll. Tolls had to be paid to travel on this road and at one time Symington had two toll houses but they no longer exist.

On 17th February 1815 a large crowd gathered at Jeanfield Toll for the execution of John Worthington, who had been charged with a series of robberies on the turnpike road between Monkton and Fenwick. He was tried in Edinburgh and then brought back to the scene of one of his crimes for execution. The crowd was entertained by practice drops until, at twenty minutes to three, Worthington was hanged. Before his burial at the Laigh Kirk in Kilmarnock, his friends lifted the lid of his coffin and covered his body with vitriol and quicklime to prevent it being stolen for dissection.

Follow the road into Symington, and at the first junction turn left into Main Street, with the Wheatsheaf Inn on your left. Ahead on the right is the War Memorial, a simple design in Peterhead granite, erected in 1921. Turn right at this memorial into Brewlands Road and park near the church. Symington is an attractive village with a number of traditional cottages.

The beautiful Norman CHURCH in Symington is one of the oldest in Scotland. The church was founded in 1160 by Symon Loccard (Lockhart), a Flemish knight with lands in Ayrshire and Lanarkshire, and whose name survives as Symington (Simon's town) in both counties. The original building had a mud floor, and parishioners brought their own seats to the services. In 1790 the walls and ceiling were plastered and the oak beams covered up. In 1797 a transept was added to the north side of the church, with a gallery above. Later a further two galleries were added to the east and west ends of the church. In 1919 the Reverend John Gage Boyd initiated major restoration work. The plaster was removed from the ceiling and walls to reveal the original oak beams. The east and west galleries were removed and the impressive Norman east window restored. The north gallery remained. This restoration work was dedicated as a memorial to the men of Symington who were killed in the First World War.

In 1950 more restoration was undertaken. Pews were removed from the chancel and a new communion table in a Norman design replaced an earlier smaller one. It was during this work that bones, believed to be those of Symon Loccard, were discovered buried under the chancel. These bones and the ashes of the Reverend John Boyd are now interred in the chancel marked by two simple crosses in the stone floor.

Symington church contains examples of beautiful stained glass windows, such as "The Risen and Glorified Lord", and the three stained glass windows under the Norman arches in the east wall depicting "The Nativity", "The Crucifixion" and "The Ascension". Today this beautiful and tranquil church can be entered through the west porch which was added in 1960 to commemorate the octocentenary.

SYMON LOCCARD. Before Robert the Bruce died in 1329 he asked Sir James Douglas to take his heart to the Holy Land. On the way there, Douglas was killed in battle against the Moors in Spain. Among the group of Scottish knights who accompanied Douglas was Sir Symon Loccard who carried the key to the casket containing Bruce's heart. The casket was brought back to Scotland and buried in Melrose Abbey, although Bruce's body had been buried in Dunfermline Abbey. The family's coat-of-arms reflects his part in this event and over time the spelling of the name changed to Lockhart.

Retrace your route from the War Memorial to the junction with Symington Road, distinguished by a bus shelter. Turn left here, and continue until you reach the junction with the busy A77. Turn left again in the direction of Kilmarnock and then immediately past the next crossroads (B730), the trees on the left form the boundary of Coodham estate.

*The **COODHAM** Estate was acquired in 1826 by Mrs William Fairlie, the widow of a wealthy Calcutta merchant banker, who was a native of Kilmarnock. She built a mansion at a cost of £20,000 and in memory of her husband, named it Williamfield. The original name is thought to be derived from 'coos' dam', a watering place for cattle, and was restored by her son James Ogilvy Fairlie, when he became the owner. J. O. Fairlie was a noted sportsman and was one of the founders of golf's Open Championship, first held at Old Prestwick in 1860 (see our companion book, Historic Prestwick).*

In 1871 the estate was bought by W. H. Houldsworth, a Scottish ironmaster and MP for Manchester. At great expense he enlarged the house by adding a splendid conservatory and a beautiful chapel. Services were held regularly which the public and the local gentry would attend. At the far side of the large artificial loch is a burial ground where a young son of Mr Houldsworth is interred. The loch itself has been since the 1840s the scene of many grand curling matches. The last outdoor playing for Ayrshire's most-prized trophy, the Eglinton Jug, took place here in 1941. There is still a lodge on the A77 and the courtyard buildings have been converted into several attractive private homes. Today, many years after the house was used as a Retreat, and many years of lying empty and neglected and plundered of everything valuable, the mansion house has been converted into prestigious living accommodation once again. Some new detached properties are also being built in the 90 acre grounds.

Take the next left turn down the slip road B7038 (signed Kilmarnock). Soon you will see a signpost for Earlston, Caprington and Gatehead on your left. Take this road. Earlston is notable for the kennels of the Eglinton Hunt on the left and its row of estate cottages. Where the road bends to the left after leaving Earlston, on the right-hand side set well back, is the entrance to Caprington Castle, a private residence.

CAPRINGTON CASTLE

Over the centuries the original tower house has been altered and extended. The castle as it appears today is the result of a restoration in 1829 which gave it its present Gothic appearance. The castle is occupied by the Cunninghame family whose ownership is thought to date back to 1462. The family is associated with the Caprington Horn, an ancient hunting horn reputed to have belonged to Old King Coil, a king who lived many centuries ago in the area. The horn, and an ancient whistle, the subject of Robert Burns' poem, The Whistle, are in the ownership of the Cunninghame family.

Continue along this road, passing beneath an attractive bridge which once carried a mineral railway, until you see Old Rome farmhouse on your left. At the road end, turn right on to the A759 towards Gatehead, cross the river and level crossing and, in the village, turn left at the Cochrane Inn.

COCHRANE is the family name of the Earls of Dundonald, who were once powerful landowners in this area. There are a number of notable members of the family, including Archibald Cochrane, 9th Earl of Dundonald (1748 - 1831), who was a pioneer scientist and industrialist, and Admiral Thomas Cochrane (1775-1860). Archibald Cochrane has been described as "the eccentric Scottish inventor whose attempts to restore prosperity to his indigent family made him an important pioneer of the chemical industry." His valiant effort to restore the family fortunes failed and he died in obscure poverty in Paris. However "to him belongs the credit of devising a commercial process of extracting coal-tar, a product upon which the industries in drugs, perfumes, explosives and dyes are now based; of helping to resolve the salt to soda problem which inhibited the expansion of the chemical industry; and of writing the first important treatise applying the principles of chemistry to agriculture." Admiral Cochrane was his son, and rose from midshipman to be Admiral of the Fleet, despite various setbacks along the way. Out of favour with the British government between 1814 and 1832, he usefully filled his time by being fully involved in the independence campaigns of Chile, Peru and Brazil. He was Vice-Admiral of Chile between 1817 and 1822. He was also Admiral of the Greek navy in their battles for independence against the Ottoman Empire. Admiral Cochrane, known in his own lifetime as The Seawolf, is the real-life person on whom two fictional characters have been based: C. S. Forester's Horatio Hornblower and Patrick O'Brien's Jack Aubrey.

Follow this road until you reach the derelict Laigh Milton mill. Park in the car park near the first entrance and looking up river you can see the LAIGH MILTON VIADUCT.

This was built in 1812, as part of the Kilmarnock and Troon Railway and is the earliest railway viaduct in the world and of considerable historical importance. When the Troon railway was absorbed into the growing national network in the late 19th Century some changes were made to its route, and a new crossing of the river was made nearer Gatehead. Consequently the viaduct passed out of use. It decayed slowly for 150 years until it was restored in 1995-96. If you wish you can walk to the viaduct along the riverside path.

Return to Gatehead by the same route. Turn right at the Cochrane Inn on to the A759 and follow this road for 2 miles or so. On the left you again pass close by the farm of Old Rome which was in the 19th Century a sizeable mining hamlet and the site of a distillery. Rome or 'room' is an old Scots word for a farm or portion of land. It was to Old Rome, where relatives of his mother lived, that Robert Burns fled in 1786 to escape the wrath of James Armour, father of Jean, who was expecting Burns' child. At this time Burns was planning to go to Jamaica as a plantation overseer but due to the success of his 'Poems Chiefly in the Scottish Dialect' ('The Kilmarnock Edition') he remained in Scotland.

Follow this road and on the right can be seen the lodge and then the attractive home farm of Fairlie House, built for Alexander Fairlie of Fairlie, who was one of the leading agricultural improvers in Ayrshire at this time. The house, which cannot be seen from the road, is noted for its many chimney stacks and is known in local parlance as Fairlie Five Lums.

FAIRLIE HOUSE

This is a delightful late Georgian mansion of 1781 - 3, with circular rooms on the main floor and fine plasterwork by Thomas Clayton of London. The builder was Francis Harvie of Irvine who, in March 1782, wrote to his brother in Halifax, "I have a gentlemans hous to do in Dundonald Mr Alexander Fairlie of Fairlie Esq which will take three thousand pounds sterling to finish it and I wrought the last year at it and this year and it will serve the next year too. I have contracted for the finishing of the house. It is thought to be the best hous in this countryside."

Continue along the A759 until reaching the junction with the B730. The land on the right was the site of a Second World War airfield.

DUNDONALD AIRFIELD

The grass airfield at Dundonald was constructed on the lands of Bogside and Kilnford farms and opened in 1940 as a relief landing ground for Prestwick. The peaty ground was made usable by the laying of beech trees beneath a layer of spoil from nearby Hillhouse quarry. In 1943 the airfield was improved with the laying of two steel matting runways. The resident unit at Dundonald was 516 SQUADRON, which provided aircraft for exercises and mock attacks with Army units training in western Scotland in preparation for the invasion of Europe. Its importance was highlighted by visits from Lord Louis Mountbatten, Chief of Combined Operations. The mixed collection of aircraft included Hurricanes, Lysanders, Mustangs and Blenheims. After D-Day, the need for such a unit declined and 516 Squadron was disbanded in December 1944. The largest aircraft to land here was a B.17 Flying Fortress of the US Army Air Force which lost its way en route to Prestwick. The runways at Dundonald were too short for it to take off again, so it had to be dismantled and taken away on trucks. After the war the airfield reverted to farmland, was subsequently developed as a chemical factory and is now an industrial estate.

At the B730 junction turn left towards Dundonald.

The first houses on the right occupy the site of Auchans House. In the 18th century this was the home of Susanna, Countess of Eglinton.

SUSANNA, COUNTESS OF EGLINTON, 1690 - 1780

The daughter of Sir Archibald Kennedy of Culzean, Susanna became the third wife of the 9th Earl of Eglinton. She was famous for her intelligence, beauty and tall, elegant figure. It was said that she kept her youthful complexion even into old age by washing her face daily with sows' milk. She was known for her patronage of the arts and had a wide knowledge of music, literature and science. She also spoke Italian, French and German. After the death of her husband in 1729 she lived at Auchans, where she concluded her dinner parties by rapping on wooden panelling. At this signal her trained rats would appear and eat the crumbs. It was at Auchans that she received

Dr Samuel Johnson and James Boswell in 1773. On their departure she embraced Johnson and said that as she was old enough to be his mother (Johnson was 64 at the time) she would adopt him as her son. Susanna died aged 90, having been a widow for 51 years. There is a beautiful portrait of Susanna at Culzean Castle.

In the village look for the signs for Dundonald Castle; the narrow access road (Winehouse Yett) is on the right opposite a bus shelter and the village's War Memorial. There is parking at the Castle Visitor Centre.

DUNDONALD CASTLE

This is a fortified tower house built for Robert II when he became King of Scotland in 1371. Robert II was the grandson of King Robert the Bruce, being the son of his daughter Marjory and her husband Walter the High Steward of Scotland whose family had occupied this site from the mid 12th century. With the accession of Robert II this family gave rise to the Stewart Dynasty that ruled Scotland and later Great Britain for 350 years. The Castle was used as a royal residence by the early Stewart kings for 150 years and it was said to be Robert II's favourite residence where he died in 1390. Ownership of the Dundonald estate passed to the Cathcarts in 1482 and later to the Wallaces in 1526 but was in ruins by the end of the 17th century. Recent excavations by Historic Scotland have revealed the remains of a succession of settlements and fortifications on the Castle Hill dating back to the Stone Age. All parts of the remains of the castle are accessible to the reasonably fit, but the visit does involve a climb of about 30 metres up a winding path to the top of the castle hill. On a clear day the hill commands very extensive views, including the Isle of Arran, the mountains of the Southern Highlands and much of the central Ayrshire plain. The Great Hall on the top floor is now roofless but the Lower Hall features a fine example of a medieval barrel-vaulted ceiling with a small dungeon below it.

A Visitor Centre owned by South Ayrshire Council and operated on their behalf by The Friends of Dundonald Castle is at the foot of the hill. It includes a café, souvenir shop and an interpretive exhibition which outlines the history of the castle and has models of earlier castles on the site. Some of the artefacts unearthed in the archaeological dig are on show as well as styles of chain mail and body armour. It is open from 10 to 5 from April to October. Dundonald Castle hosts weddings, musical events, Medieval Days and has been used as a film venue. More information can be found at www.dundonaldcastle.org.uk

From the castle car park return to the narrow village street and turn right. At the far end of the village, the parish church is prominent on the right.

DUNDONALD CHURCH

This traditional stone church built at the top of the village Main Street in 1804 is on the site of an earlier church. The tower dates from 1841, and its spire contains a clock. The chancel, added in 1906-10, contains a fine stained glass window depicting the Last Supper by Henry Dearle.

The churchyard contains some interesting old carved grave stones.

A second church built in 1843, down a lane opposite this church, was the Free Church. Its first minister was the Reverend Thomas Burns, the nephew of Robert Burns. It is now the parish church hall.

Just past the church turn right off the B730 on to the hill road, Old Loans Road. Follow this over the top of Dundonald Hill, with a breath-taking panorama of the Firth of Clyde. In this area there are ancient earthworks including a vitrified fort. There is a parking place on the right of the road if you wish to stop.

From south (left) to north, the view from DUNDONALD HILL encompasses Turnberry Point, Ailsa Craig, with Arran ahead, and Lady Isle between Troon and Arran. Features on the coast range from the windfarm above West Kilbride, through the dunes at Stevenston and Irvine, past Troon, Ayr, the Heads of Ayr and back again to Turnberry Point. The Paps of Jura can be seen beyond the northern end of Arran on a clear day.

LADY ISLE

This is a small island three miles from Troon, which is now a bird sanctuary. No landings are allowed without permission. There is a huge colony of lesser black-backed and herring gulls, while other birds to be seen include roseate tern, greater black-backed gull, eider, cormorant, shag, oystercatcher, purple sandpiper, dunlin and turnstone. Seals can often be found in the vicinity. There is a lighthouse on Lady Isle, built in 1903 and still in use. It is a white concrete tower with buttress supports and an external spiral stairway, and replaces one of two beacons set up by the town of Glasgow c.1776. The other beacon survives, as does a basic shelter built c.1958 by the Scottish Society for the Protection of Wild Birds.

The road continues down, passing Highgrove House, a house of 1916, now a hotel, which takes full advantage of the views, to a roundabout at Loans.

At this roundabout it is possible to turn right, and as an alternative route return to Troon via BARASSIE. *The name originated from a local farm and burn, but it had been known as New Kilmarnock in the 1830s when well-to-do families from Kilmarnock* *came here for a holiday, and built villas. Over the years Barassie has grown with the development of many new houses.*

At the roundabout go straight ahead, passing on the left a standing stone and on the right the Muirhead housing estate and the former staff houses and present playing fields of Marr College. After a mile, as the road rises to cross the railway, the entrance to Marr College itself, with its distinctive green dome, is on the right.

Charles Kerr MARR was born in 1855 in Troon and was the third son of a ship's captain. He first became apprenticed to a Troon coal merchant but moved from there to Glasgow and then London where he ultimately became a partner in Hall Blyth and Co. where he developed their export trade. In time the firm became one of the largest shipping charterers in the country. Depots were established throughout the world and his work gave him the reason and opportunity to travel. He was a lover of the arts and music. In his retirement he spent a good part of each year in Scotland fishing and shooting. He died in 1919 with no heirs. Many of his closest friends believed him to be a bachelor; in truth he had been married but his wife Agnes had died very young. He seldom spoke of his loss but he is buried in Cathcart Cemetery, Glasgow beside her. He left around £300,000 upon his death to the people of Troon.

MARR COLLEGE

Troon's secondary school was built in 1928-30, to plans of John Arthur. Its construction was funded by the C. K. Marr Educational Trust. It cost nearly £240,000 to build, but its opening was delayed until 1935, due to prolonged discussions about its  *relationship to the county-wide educational system.*

The original building is symmetrical, in a classical manner, and, with its dome, forms a prominent landmark. Many of the associated buildings, including the gate pillars, and the attractive lodge, are also by Arthur. The opening ceremony was performed by the Marquis of Lothian, with Sir Alexander Walker in the chair. If, as rumour suggests, Joachim von Ribbentrop was present, as a guest of Walker, some of Lord Lothian's remarks on the political situation in Germany become additionally pointed. In 2010 discussions began about moving the school to a new building. There is also the C. K. Marr Educational Trust which provides financial support for people who live in Troon or Loans to attend university or college.

Where the road crosses the railway was the site of Troon's station on the Ayr to Glasgow line, opened in 1840. A loop was built to bring the railway nearer the town centre and the new station was opened in 1892. The old station was converted to a goods station until it was dismantled some years later.

Turn left at the first set of traffic lights and follow the road (St Meddan's Street) passing the Catholic Church on the left.

OUR LADY OF THE ASSUMPTION AND ST MEDDAN

Troon's impressive Roman Catholic Church was built in 1910 - 11 to designs by the architect Reginald Fairlie. The style is bold Scots Gothic Revival, into which Fairlie has packed a variety of details, such as the crown spire, based on Linlithgow Church, and the five-sided apse, a motif from the Church of the Holy Rood, Stirling. Fairlie has blended these disparate historical elements to create a church which is firmly of its own time and one of the best in Scotland of its date. The spacious and simply detailed interior is equally striking.
The church is usually open during the day.

ST MEDDAN'S PARISH CHURCH

St Meddan's is graced by a beautiful east window representing Christ's miracle, the Raising of Jairus' daughter (Mark 5: 35-43). The window was designed by William Smith of London in 1892 and this is believed to be his only surviving work. The donor was James Gillies, a wealthy coal exporter and one-time Provost of Troon. In 2008 the window was placed fourth in the RCAHMS list of 100 Treasured Places. Recognition of its quality led to its being restored, almost the whole cost being met by the congregation. The meticulous conservation was carried out by Moira Malcolm of Rainbow Glass.

Continue along St Meddan's Street, passing the churches of St Meddan's (on the right) and Portland (on the left) to its junction with South Beach, and the car park where the trail started.

FURTHER READING

Most of the following, many of which are out-of-print, can be found in Troon Library, as can many general texts on broader aspects of Ayrshire history. Additionally, much more information and many photographs, old and new, can be found on locally maintained websites. The local family history society is Troon @ Ayrshire Family History Society. The best recent book on Troon is I. M. Mackintosh, Old Troon and District: An Historical Account, first published in 1969, and re-published in a revised edition in 1972. James H. Gillespie's Dundonald: A Contribution to Parochial History (Glasgow, 1939) is a traditional parish history which remains pertinent and valuable. There is nothing similar for Symington.

The area's smuggling heritage is well served by two books by Frances Wilkins: Strathclyde's Smuggling Story (Kidderminster, 1992) and The Loans Smugglers (Ayr, AANHS, 2008), while Gavin Ewart and Denys Pringle, eds., Dundonald Castle Excavations 1986-1993 (Edinburgh, 2004), as vol. 26 pts 1 & 2 of the Scottish Archaeological Journal, is a comprehensive account of the development of this important building. For the Kilmarnock & Troon Railway, Roland Paxton's An Engineering Assessment of the Kilmarnock & Troon Railway 1807-1846, in Andy Guy & Jim Rees, eds., Early Railways, London, 2001, is thorough, and puts the line into its contemporary setting. David McClure, ed., Ayrshire in the Age of Improvement, re-prints William Fullarton's late 18th century account of Ayrshire's agriculture (Ayr, AANHS, 2002), while Paul Crankshaw and Neil Dickson's Old Rome: Hiding Burns to Hidden Hamlet, in Ayrshire Notes 37 (2009) is an in-depth study of this small hamlet. Finally, a novel - Mick Jackson's The Underground Man (1997, paperback 2007), based on the life of the 5th Duke of Portland.

Ayrshire Archaeological and Natural History Society

Publications in print

Burns and the Sugar Plantocracy of Ayrshire (Graham)

Masters of Ballantrae (Hunter)

Dr John Taylor, Chartist: Ayrshire Revolutionary (Fraser)

The Early Transatlantic Trade of Ayr, 1640-1730 (Graham & Barclay)

Historic Ayr: a guide for visitors

Historic Alloway: Village and Countryside

Historic Prestwick and its Surroundings

Robert Adam in Ayrshire (Sanderson)

Tattie Howkers (Holmes)

Street Names of Ayr (Close)

The Port of Ayr, 1727-1780 (Graham)

Ayrshire in the Age of Improvement (ed. McClure)

Tolls and Tacksmen (McClure)

Armstrong's map of Ayrshire, 1775 (6 sheets)

Available from the Publications Distribution Manager:
Ronald Brash, 10 Robsland Avenue, Ayr KA7 2RW